TRIOS

IRREVERSIBLE TERCETS

IN LINES OF DIMINISHING

LENGTH

MIKE SILVERTON

Portions of this work appeared in the journal *Exacting Clam*, in slightly different form.

© 2022 by Mike Silverton

All Rights Reserved.

Set in Janson Text with LaTeX.

ISBN: 978-1-952386-51-0 (paperback)
Library of Congress Control Number: 2022948629

Sagging Meniscus Press
Montclair, New Jersey
saggingmeniscus.com

*I dedicate these poems to Lithium,
the atomic number of which
is three.*

TRIOS

I

Trios are not to be confused with ceviche (suhVEEchay). Trios are inedible. Trios consist, among other features, of targets. (Alternately, trios consist of, among other features, targets.)

II

Refrigerate. Reduce scallops to tears, with a thin slice of weevil. Include agencies, soviets, covens, jirgas and a peshmerga or two. They do what they can, thinking it's never enough.

III

We remark chaos skulking amidst a necessary obscurity. Also kanakas abusing ukuleles.

IV

Ceramic tiles: petite vault doors
enclosing toy pandas,
dreaming.

V

Excellence enhanced with lemon zest, had crazy-ass gas
a thoughtful thing been, stage left, pantry
moths.

VI

Plenty of hither to carry us thither, waddling along with Buonaparte's mob like jumped-up scarabs in tatty
duds.

VII

Geraniums call kitsch to mind. Wound-oozy martyrs approve. To be synchronous with plumbing's fluids, looks of anticipation, clouds doing what clouds do, thanks to you, comrade sky.

VIII

X endures, Y not so much. What next, the plug wonders snug in its jug
and so do you. Is it possible we're on the wrong alp?
Turning around's an option.

IX

Tree surgeon in error lynched. Bon chance deposits where Mother Lode lodges.
I shall too soon halt and degrade, nurturing illusions
of moist effusions.

X

When off an edge a pilgrim stumbles, nasals oboe dirge morose, cello, tuba, trombone euphonious. It's at the bottom percussion awaits.

XI

Aflame the ballroom where I thumped my bamboula,
opaque with smoke, spattered Ma
zola.

XII

Question accountancy! Investigative poetry demands it! Suns set,
onslaughts befall. Your years differ from mine,
beginning at the orphanage.

XIII

Heard the one about the Senegalese merchant?
Seems his camels are strangers.
Strange camels.

XIV

Above all else (hands to breast), Mother of God! They say I shall hurt me!
Yes, they do say it! The deed will remain
in the family aisle.

XV

Respighi gnaws his fedora. The poet declines
to water seedlings. The future lies.
Ahead, I mean.

XVI

As any sniper knows, success is the carom's best friend. How less than fulfilling
to aspire to the heavens imagined through a ceiling that falls
on one's face. Moon. Crickets. Stars.

XVII

In discarding oneself one could aim for the trash, achieving thereby,
of courtesy and comity, a comely
simultaneity.

XVIII

Kit Carson's dead. Because we have our wisdom teeth
we understand that these things
happen.

XIX

I seem the buffoon in Donald Duck slippers? Is it, again, the vision thing? Is it bad judgment, the hours spent quacking, dreaming duck dreams, seeing the stars
as eggs to be cracked?

XX

This leg I'm on might be my last. It's also tough on elderly voles. How to queue? By size? By diploma? As little drips monsoons begin, no more alarming than ziti al dente.

XXI

Guillaume Apollinaire, Guillaume de Machaut, Billy the Kid,
William B. Williams, utility
bill.

XXII

Colleen, my colleen, o'demeanor kayacky, your features I bathe in dancing confetti,
the kind one dumps from high office
windows.

XXIII

Bus-shat baggage (peristaltic chortle). What brings you here,
the prize or the promise? Did anyone
warn you?

XXIV

Starlight fashions impressions with long fingers. Debris clutters unregistered canyons. Cadence marks time.

XXV

Certain afflictions simply are. Certain
attractions include me
teors.

XXVI

Snakes of more than ordinary brilliance dwell among mongooses,
in the main, uneasily. Fact: hedgehogs are
stupid.

XXVII

Of no particular discernment, mayhem operates
under canopies, in arenas and, oh,
why not, ogre depots.

XXVIII

All at sea in anomie? Wondering what it's all about? Install an arm
ature.

XXIX

I won't dance, you can't make me. I also won't bark.
And I wish to remind that magicians
are people.

XXX

Disregard questionable emotions. Be amiable. Jockey for a favorable outcome. Pause to consider décor.

XXXI

Inquiry is especially fruitful in divination by turds. While it's obvious I've just spoken, I shall soon eat my vocabulary. Am busy sorting condiments.

XXXII

The optimist's daughters are largely stationary. But when they step out in their perfect slippers golden coupons spring up from the earth.

XXXIII

If one should enter a tree shredder could we call it chop
suicide, or would that sound too much
like food?

XXXIV

Spend your days aloft with a latex-free familiar. Place
your legs in God's hands and turn on
the shaking alarm.

XXXV

Bedside assistants and swimming-pool golf await the faithful. And jumbo thermometers. Mounting brackets included.

XXXVI

Recent additions include a nose-hair stimulant, a Krakatoa replica, irresolute geese and non-fungible mists.

XXXVII

Your creamy white head turns pink as
the night grows cooler and
slices easily.

XXXVIII

Create a maze. Distribute piñatas. Bombard with bowling balls,
rocks, paper weights, whatever's handy,
take notes.

XXXIX

Kick back, unwind, entertain the Onanism Clique with cautionary maxims. "Idle hands are playthings . . .",
and so on.

XL

While I wouldn't call myself a great cook, I simply can't stop. I poached my hand overnight, I mean Friday night, and the kids didn't smell a thing.

XLI

My memories taste like pipe cleaners. Autumn leaves and dollops occupy the slots.

XLII

"Sutures!" she cried, floating across the moors. "Or else!"
Citizens! I'm writing poems on everything!
In ink!

XLIII

And that's not all, I said, and jumped. Thank you! Next! Hey,
droopy drawers, upon my boughs the birds,
they don't loiter.

XLIV

Literati swoon at the thought of a sestina and
who's been riding a bike
in here?

XLV

The poet has an eel by the tail. If not quite true,
it is at least clearly stat
ed.

XLVI

Hi, Betty. Hi, Martha. How about that Grand Vizier, whacking the Madonna around like that?

XLVII

To the sentient tablecloth the dining room ceiling is heaven. An ominous passerby bursts in on the dinner party
and spills wine.

XLVIII

Deciduous police all have wide eyes and some have tiny hearing aids. And sparrow feathers in their chapeaux. They avoid sunlight.

XLIX

You cannot fully appreciate digestion
until you walk barefoot
in shit.

L

Something somewhere lies in wait. And thin-soup
manifestos. And distant coups
d'etoile.

LI

For further study: the inaudible thumps of eyelid blinks,
a standing rib roast's
destiny.

LII

Brace yourself for an intervention, Edna. Ethnicity is entirely felicitous, like fart bubbles
in the bath.

LIII

Digame, hombre, where are the snoods? The viaducts, gone, the temples, gone, and as I just learned, passion subsides
at room temperature.

LIV

The best poetry resembles carrots flying out doors. I board
Airscoop Destiny perchance to an award, and there
goes Popeye in a petal-fragrant sky.

LV

Drop everything. Fine-tune your vision. Calibrate your hearing.
Savor the universe in a dozen ways
or less.

LVI

Commodore Perry issues three suggestions: avoid waste,
observe equanimity (queen among postures),
and remain vertical.

LVII

We've just enough feet to carry us there. Carious? Where?
You're probably wondering, is this person
a dentist?

LVIII

Lady Murasaki pitches cherry-blossom pies
at narcoleptic ronin striking
yam-like poses.

LIX

Pensées, permafrost, walnuts.
Aim nozzle at sky and
squeeze.

LX

Stuck to this or that moment, the poet
lectures in disheveled
triplicate.

LXI

Poetry recommends sniffing tear gas
the better to grasp un
willingness.

LXII

A chipped incisor in a pasta carbonara? A bent fork in a tiramisu? Is that even likely?
No!

LXIII

There exist turns of speech which, if not quite metaphors,
are sufficiently allusive to require
curiosity.

LXIV

A puff of air installs desire in a cadaver. The morgue becomes a tourist attraction.

LXV

Taking in vistas through dainty pink toes. Poetry!
From pillar to post to any
where!

LXVI

I call her Electricidad on Wednesdays. On weekends, Zephyr. As an endearment, Little Snotfish.

LXVII

The poet notes a viper's proximity and – pop! pop! pop! –
breaks out in logorrhea. It proves oddly
effective.

LXVIII

Many canaries live in cages. Most buzzards don't.
And there lies a sand dollar, alone
and wistful.

LXIX

Dogs acquire ticks by chance. As for me,
I'm flying to Capri by way of
trebuchet.

LXX

I'm prepared to discuss unintelligibility as soon as
you tell me why your eyeballs
do that thing.

LXXI

Recent nightmare: Pseudopods trampling lint
gathered from virgins'
navels.

LXXII

Find me a nice obelisk. Stick me on top. I'll be
ornamental, like a flesh-tone
stove pipe.

LXXIII

All within sight and beyond, refurnished.
The galaxies croon, Bring
us more.

LXXIV

Forty-thousand subjects shat tourmalines, for
the king had power. He rolled
off a cloud.

LXXV

An anarchist tied my shoelaces together. It's a problem, scanning prospects, trying to walk away.

LXXVI

"The sound unuttered lives deep within the breast." Flat-faced
from chastisement with a cast-iron skillet ought
at least to warrant an ouch.

LXXVII

Selective breeding has me here, fishing with
Little Willy. A nibble only.
A poetic sigh.

LXXVIII

A vaguely familiar tune is like an elusive flavor.
It's not interesting unless
it is.

LXXIX

Briefly, Melpomene, Practical Poetry
celebrates good hy
giene.

LXXX

Prancing clams are improbable. Snow White's psoriasis is inappropriate. Supplementation with vitamins
is often unnecessary.

LXXXI

Foxtrotting on an oil slick, I mimic
a gigolo with contrarian
urges.

LXXXII

Moiré yard goods give me the vapors,
especially when they elude
detection.

LXXXIII

When I deposit my poet's hat on my head,
you might think to ask, is that really
a Stetson?

LXXXIV

The gods sniff and compare us to posterity. The gods
perforce must acknowledge their
complicity.

LXXXV

Let us discover whom these chunks belong to. The joke's
on who? On whom? Later, in the lagoon,
we scout for sequins.

LXXXVI

This poem proposes gluing you to your briefs, yet your
attention turns wayward. And for this you
expect gratitude.

LXXXVII

Let's look into a head. Aha! A diorama! And little bumps!
The key to understanding also starts
my car.

LXXXVIII

As a sly anonymity XO appears as hugs and kisses on friendly correspond
ence.

LXXXIX

Client claims he fails eternally. Technician replaces fan belt, fluids and longings.

XC

Quivering accelerates when hussars
congeal and strong words
melt artillery.

XCI

Descending in a gondola, Jupiter scowls, especially at those engorging on fudge in white clapboard mansions.

XCII

Grains of rice enclosing tiny villages exist! Grains of rice
with amnesia exist! Meissen grains of rice
on fancy mantels exist!

XCIII

In 1923 I was utterly inarticulate. In 2023 I can say plethora twenty-three times fast.

XCIV

My bile duct is stuffed with stolen kisses. The man who beguiles beetles
cannot make this claim. Legions kicking cans down roads
cannot make this claim.

XCV

Aesop's mountains are at last in labor.
Best to alert the frolicking
condors.

XCVI

Seeking the divine under blue tarpaulins calls
tent revivals to
mind.

XCVII

Unfaithful husbands avoid mirrors that reflect them as rakes
at the edge of an abyss, with cuckolds
poised to push.

XCVIII

In the matter of realpolitik sonatas take no position.
With respect to terrorists the minor key
opens doors.

XCIX

Shmuel changed his name to Ipanema. Sounds less Jewish. He believes that Flushing is indoor plumbing's birthplace.

C

Acquiring trees to learn their ways devolves to bonsai
and permanent drought. A green thumb
requires medical attention.

CI

Mercurial, marmoreal, rigorous, frivolous, a poem should smell like your favorite restaurant.

CII

In a front-row seat, in garments of my own design, I monitor debris.
A recent near-miss, an ingenue's jaw bone,
fills me with hope.

CIII

Not all passageways lead to rewards. I know of one that takes you to a blue tarpaulin over
a dire outcome.

CIV

The poet addresses his virtuous twin: Your ensemble is wanting. Much of it rubs off. With one eye closed I can smell your pretentions at twenty meters.

CV

I discovered a culvert under the bed,
behind it a leg covered
in lips.

CVI

I like to think of fans twinkling in the distance
like a little flotilla bound for
Cockaigne.

CVII

Repurposing blue tarpaulins as novelty housing
posits need vis-à-vis
scale.

CVIII

I sing of the plumb bob in honey-lustrous brass
and of its devotion and un
flinching gaze.

CIX

Encourage everyone you know to snap off bits.
We need to work at being
less.

CX

Rabbits that rattle like pebbles disquiet elephants.
Dreams founder when poetry defers
to decibels.

CXI

Be alert to spontaneity. Some of it's hostile. Whatever it seems, feign
interest. For example, if I should sound symphonic,
look behind the draperies.

CXII

Whether lyrical, angular, licentious, mercurial, glacial, tropical, glandular, opaque, specious or topical, any randomly chosen trio's ancillary possibilities could fill an in-ground swimming pool.

CXIII

Poetry acknowledges topographical oddities. Poetry acknowledges laundry cults. Poetry steps out for a smoke and vanishes. Poetry moonlights as a paperhanger.

CXIV

A poem winces when readers of the wrong sort stuff wads
under its affect. Moments in the afterlife
are similarly troublesome.

CXV

Surely this is an enchantment. (It is.) (I thought so.) Observing
events through holes in the head,
less than ideal.

CXVI

That's no python, that's my dachshund,
Little Twenty-Mule
Team.

CXVII

I meet a girl. We exchange smiles. Hers
doesn't fit but it tastes
good.

CXVIII

A drooling poltroon evades an ectoplasmic silhouette auditing a mosh pit. It's poetry's duty to explain.

CXIX

Be of easy mind, bugs. You're bouncing up and down
because Earth trembles when I write
poems.

CXX

Dear Aunt Edna, thanks for the
barbells. They fell in
the toilet.

CXXI

I was one of several neophytes up to our philtra in holy water. I dreamt
I was at bat with a prince of the Church's femur.
Full count. I anticipate a slider.

CXXII

Does a shy, philosophical eruption suggest
to a nameless street a spirit of
fled recognition?

CXXIII

A properly crafted poem should call to mind chalk-white buttocks
floating in a stew as sloe-eyed spirits whisper spells,
here and anywhere.

CXXIV

Were we in a rockslide I wouldn't question your gestures,
but as we enjoy a more leisurely state
I think I'll take my leave.

CXXV

The park bench I'm on has knuckles. The one across has feathers.
If I'm carried off, may it be in a sitting position.
I'd like onlookers to wonder.

CXXVI

A roc's egg sits atop a flame. It bursts, disfiguring a metropolis. Artifice, ruse or stratagem?

CXXVII

The best place to stand when Brother Thanatos drops by is in front of the bull's-eye. Brother Thanatos admires self-effacement.

CXXVIII

I long for a wall so stout as to stop those who ask, How can we proceed with our noses thus pressed against a wall so stout?

CXXIX

Don't go! Lounge, rather, and savor the language. If you hold your breath and remain very still perhaps you'll hear it colliding.

CXXX

Translucent, benevolent, no sharp corners,
one poet's muse is another's
ice cube.

CXXXI

We note a homemaker in a randomly selected cottage kneading a wad. It probably isn't dangerous.

CXXXII

It requires poetry to extract the ripest metaphors from
the narrowest cracks. As to bludgeons,
Cosmic Fillip delivers the goods.

CXXXIII

Figment, to you or the pillow one finds himself driven
with diminishing returns. Dreamboats
founder.

CXXXIV

Strap the elk to your ride's red roof and drive west fast.
Plan as you evade the light when to schedule
an eye exam.

CXXXV

An able-bodied seaman jigs into a plaza, jigs yet farther into a bay. Questioned, he answers, "I require attention."

CXXXVI

Pewter Rabbit is an imposter.
The valley beyond is
occupied.

CXXXVII

Try looking like something enticing or maybe a nuisance, like a hog in the orange juice, then observe how the white man shakes his cocktails!

CXXXVIII

As maman used to say, Arrête toi when ready. Oscar Mayer, the coo-coo chasseur, fires when his dander's up. The moon takes note, goes into eclipse.

CXXXIX

Proceeding through brow-high asparagus we come upon a unicycle, a fisherman's friend, a larder, a velodrome, overwrought iron, Lincoln Logs, a tangerine, binoculars, a TV dinner, an exit.

CXL

"¡Ai de mi!" I hear you cry. I hear you sobbing "¡Sancta Maria!" and out of your skin you fly with spare parts, and from the dark bedroom, "I feel so much better."

CXLI

As the poet achieves full viscosity, his sunrise fontanelles call to mind the music of gummy machinery. A salute, when appropriate, to recipes for bicycle cheese.

CXLII

Spells of wishful thinking, useful as snowshoes fending off rockets.
True Believers in distress recuperate on guano,
heaped.

CXLIII

Whimpers within a sculptor's darkened studio:
lost wax figure on casting's
eve.

CXLIV

I blush to confess it, I stuffed a Dalmatian with kelp. That's also me imposing postage fines. Oh, Destiny, how I betray us with petit-bourgeois distractions!

CXLV

I'd like this poem to sound like an andiron clopping an evasive tortoise.
When the poem bares its teeth the cooperative reader
should envision headstones.

CXLVI

The night stores its softer weapons under a carpet. The planets stand, as if arranged,
like mama's little almonds, one moment beautiful,
the next, much the same.

CXLVII

Listen! That's History tiptoeing past my door! A semaphore signals for something less vague. Poetry's a kind of legerdemain
with indigestible parts.

CXLVIII

Fascists shed tears that resemble nose pickings. It remains to repair inaccuracies with incorruptible moving parts.

CXLIX

There's the cottage stuffed with the path I took. There's the Dungeness crab goo
I mentioned. And there's the wound-up face
thumping in the gazebo.

CL

My memories of vistas are noticeably compressed though not nearly as much as the brioche I just sat on. So here I stand on a windswept balcony trying to forget an indoor gaffe.

CLI

In the Ethics Lost-and-Found one cheers the pearl fishers who've swept into view.
It reminds one of Stanislav's Rebus having reappeared from under
the confusion of Orientalist bric-a-brac.

CLII

One is but a thread of pleasure-seeking phlegm a little fishy on the tongue, unrequited, sour, or so they report. The question asks
where saltiness went.

CLIII

Where victors consoled the smitten foe, even the injured
rose from their litters to join the commiseration
(when chivalry meant something).

CLIV

In a reality in which oysters occur in absentia we remain unused to household rubbish issuing recommendations. And yet when the phone rings we answer it.

CLV

Reader, I so envy your smile I want to run outdoors and empty bluebirds. I never squat without coming up with stuff.

CLVI

I train gloves to fly. A knack for yeomanry helps.
My song, Ataturk's Nut Shop, consists
of many peeps.

CLVII

Even or Odd? The player gets ten beans, and with each bean, a grey cloak. The player put his or her beans in an oven – any oven. If the beans vanish, the player prepares for outcomes.

CLVIII

Plump and fueled, lovelier even than rivets in rows,
side-effects like wandering
jewels....

CLIX

Where feathers appear from
nowhere, poetry
smiles.

CLX

Daylights filter through privet. Existence determines which is brighter.
A skeptic questions existence's existence. A candle
burns at someone's both ends.

CLXI

Join me at the Alternating Monuments where aspects cast shadows on a backwater toolbox's mainstream chanson.

CLXII

Nothing puts me quite so elsewhere as a riot.
The poop deck's the last to go
under.

CLXIII

How blue our sky! (Yes, *that* one.) How like
St. George's wattles the picture-
peppered clouds!

CLXIV

Begone, wretched persimmon! I elevate my thoughts!
My amour-propre sweeps gloom
like a broom!

CLXV

A sufficient number of hailstones bouncing off a similar abundance of keyboards would eventually produce tercets. Poetry in the abstract is at least as irrefutable as the best metaphysics has to offer.

CLXVI

As a child I learned not to fondle flames. The guardian angel in my nose tells me when something's
wrong.

CLXVII

The audience arrives with five styles of potato. "Old-Time Sex in a Frangipani Forest," has long been a hit; likewise "Droving One's Acne off to Seattle."

CLXVIII

Pastel highlights flicker, suitors gurgle endearments,
fermentation bubbles vert
ically.

CLXIX

An actuary's ferret eats zeros: outcomes neither here nor there. A mailbox opens. Catalogs.

Mike Silverton's poetry appeared in the late '60s and '70s in numerous periodicals and anthologies. He produced poetry readings for The New School for Social Research, New York's municipal radio station, WNYC, and Pacifica Radio's WBAI, KPFA, and KPFK. One glaring regret: Mike had arranged to record Frank O'Hara on the week in which he was killed, fateful weekend intervening, by a dune buggy.

Mike's music writing, centering on modernist classical, has appeared in *Fanfare*, his own *LaFolia.com*, and elsewhere. He has also reviewed high-end audio hardware for *Fanfare*, *The Absolute Sound* and *The StereoTimes.com*.

In early 2002, he and his wife Lee relocated to an 1842 house and barn in Midcoast Maine, where he indulged an interest in assemblage of an etiolated Dada persuasion, resulting in several works in a group show at The Center for Maine Contemporary Art in Rockport, and a one-man show at Belfast's Aarhus Gallery.

Recently he has been a regular contributor to the quarterly literary journal *Exacting Clam*. In 2022, his collection *Anvil on a Shoestring* was published by Sagging Meniscus.

www.ingramcontent.com/pod-product-compliance
Lightning Source LLC
Chambersburg PA
CBHW061118170426
43199CB00027B/2961